Fun with
CHINESE
Cooking

Frances Lee

PowerKiDS
press

New York

Published in 2010 by The Rosen Publishing Group, Inc.
29 East 21st Street, New York, NY 10010

U.S. Editor: Kara Murray

Photo Credits: All images by Marco Lanza and Walter Mericchi.

Library of Congress Cataloging-in-Publication Data

Lee, Frances, 1971–
  Fun with Chinese cooking / Frances Lee.
     p. cm. — (Let's get cooking!)
  Includes index.
  ISBN 978-1-4358-3453-8 (library binding) — ISBN 978-1-4358-3475-0 (pbk.) —
ISBN 978-1-4358-3476-7 (6-pack)
  1. Cookery, Chinese—Juvenile literature. 2. Food habits—China—Juvenile literature. I. Title.
  TX724.5.C5L435 2010
  641.5951—dc22

                                  2009010337

Printed in China

Contents

Introduction

China is one of the world's oldest civilizations, and its **cuisine** is famous around the world. This cookbook teaches you how to make

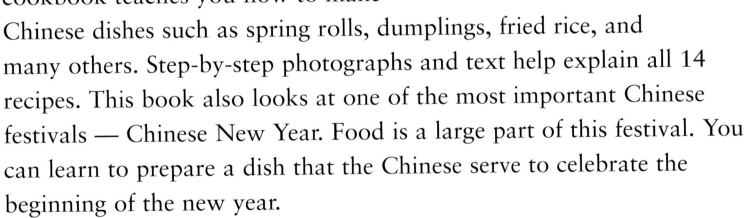

Chinese dishes such as spring rolls, dumplings, fried rice, and many others. Step-by-step photographs and text help explain all 14 recipes. This book also looks at one of the most important Chinese festivals — Chinese New Year. Food is a large part of this festival. You can learn to prepare a dish that the Chinese serve to celebrate the beginning of the new year.

When cooking, you should always have an adult with you in the kitchen to help. Many of the tools used to prepare these recipes and others can be dangerous. Always be very careful when using a knife or a stove.

Spring Rolls

Spring rolls are many people's favorite **appetizer**, and they are not too hard to make at home. They can be made ahead of time and kept in the refrigerator until you are ready to cook them. You may change the filling to suit your own tastes.

Utensils

CHOPSTICKS

SKILLET OR
FRYING PAN

WOODEN
SPOON

BOWLS

1 Place a large frying pan on the stove over high heat. Add 2 tablespoons of oil. Stir-fry the turnip or cabbage and carrots until they are lightly cooked.

2 Add the water chestnuts and bamboo shoots to the pan and stir until they are heated.

3 Add the shrimp, sugar, soy sauce, salt, and pepper to the pan and mix well. Pour the ingredients into a large bowl and leave to cool.

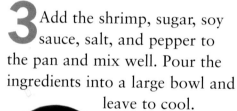

TIPS & TRICKS

Spring rolls must be fried in hot oil to be crispy. If the oil is not hot enough, the rolls will be soggy. If it is too hot, the rolls will burn. To test if the oil is hot enough, take a bit of bread and put it in the oil. If the bread sizzles and browns, the oil is hot enough. Boiling oil can splatter and cause burns. Never use it to fry anything unless an adult helps you.

5 Prepare the spring roll skins for filling as explained on the package. Place 2 tablespoons of the mixture in the center of each skin. Take two opposite ends of the skin and fold one over the other, using the egg like glue to seal the edges. Wet the other two ends with the egg and roll into a log shape. Repeat until all the mixture is used.

4 Crack open the egg and beat it in a small bowl using chopsticks or a fork.

6 Heat the remaining oil in a deep pan until very hot. Slip the spring rolls into the oil and fry until golden brown, turning frequently so that they brown evenly all over.

7 Using a slotted spoon, remove the cooked rolls from the pan and place on paper towels to absorb the extra oil. Serve hot.

Ingredients

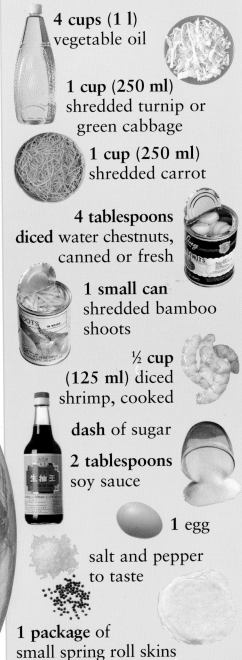

- **4 cups (1 l)** vegetable oil
- **1 cup (250 ml)** shredded turnip or green cabbage
- **1 cup (250 ml)** shredded carrot
- **4 tablespoons diced** water chestnuts, canned or fresh
- **1 small can** shredded bamboo shoots
- **½ cup (125 ml) diced** shrimp, cooked
- **dash** of sugar
- **2 tablespoons** soy sauce
- **1 egg**
- salt and pepper to taste
- **1 package** of small spring roll skins

Shrimp and Pork Dumplings

These little dumplings are a dim sum dish. In **Cantonese** cuisine, dim sum is usually served in the late morning or early afternoon. A dim sum meal consists of a variety of steamed and deep-fried foods, such as dumplings and mini spring rolls, and ends with custard tarts.

Utensils

LARGE BOWL

WOODEN SPOON

GRATER

STEAMER

LARGE WOK

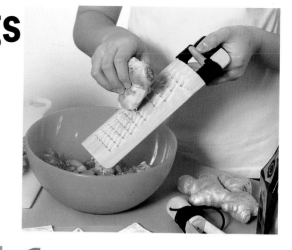

1 Combine all the ingredients, except the **wonton** wrappers, in a large bowl and mix until it is smooth and without lumps.

TIPS & TRICKS

Before steaming, cover the dumplings with a slightly wet cloth so the wonton skin does not dry out and become tough. After steaming, brush a little oil on the underside of the dumpling to keep it from sticking to the plate.

2 Place 1 **heaping** tablespoon of filling into the middle of a wonton skin and fold the corners together. Use a little cold water to make the corners stick. Repeat until all the dumplings are made.

3 Fill a wok or large pot with water and bring to a boil. Put the dumplings in the steamer and place it over the pot of boiling water. Cover the steamer with the lid.

4 Steam for about 20 minutes or until the meat is cooked through. Serve the dim sum warm with some light soy sauce and sliced ginger or chili sauce.

Ingredients

1 tablespoon grated ginger

1 pound (450 g) finely **minced** pork

1 cup (250 ml) chopped shelled shrimp

1 tablespoon light soy sauce

½ tablespoon sesame oil

½ tablespoon sugar

1 egg

1 tablespoon cornstarch

½ teaspoon white pepper

1 package wonton skins, thawed

Sweet Corn Soup with Crabmeat

Drinks are not usually served at a Chinese family meal. Instead, people usually serve a bowl of soup. Soups have long been a part of Chinese cuisine. In fact, a Chinese poem written over 2,200 years ago talks about a person eating a "sour and bitter soup."

1 Place the chicken stock in a large pot and bring it to a boil. Add the corn and sliced ginger and simmer over low heat for about 15 minutes.

Ingredients

6 cups (1.5 l) chicken stock (made with hot water and a bouillon cube)

1 cup (250 ml) corn kernels

8 ounces (250 g) cooked crabmeat

3–4 slices fresh ginger

1 egg white

1 teaspoon sesame oil

1 tablespoon light soy sauce

dash of salt

2 teaspoons cornstarch

dash of white pepper

dash of sugar

2 green onions, chopped

1 tablespoon cold water

To save time, use frozen or canned corn. The slices of ginger add flavor to the soup, but be sure to remove them before serving. Their flavor is too strong to eat. Green onions also have a strong taste. If you do not like them, leave them out of the soup.

2 While the corn is simmering, mix the cornstarch, soy sauce, sesame oil, salt, pepper, sugar, and water in a small bowl until it becomes a smooth paste.

3 Pour the soy sauce paste into the soup. Turn the heat up to medium and stir until the soup starts to boil.

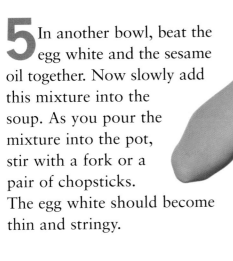

4 Use a spoon to add the crabmeat to the soup. Stir gently so that you do not get splashed with the boiling soup. Simmer for 5 more minutes.

6 Use a slotted spoon to remove the slices of ginger from the soup. Sprinkle the soup with green onions and extra pepper. Serve hot.

5 In another bowl, beat the egg white and the sesame oil together. Now slowly add this mixture into the soup. As you pour the mixture into the pot, stir with a fork or a pair of chopsticks. The egg white should become thin and stringy.

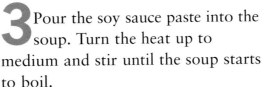

Utensils

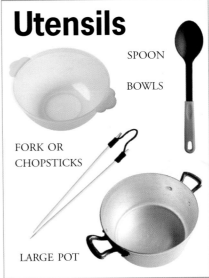

SPOON

BOWLS

FORK OR CHOPSTICKS

LARGE POT

Four-Color Soup

This healthy vegetable dish can be made even more filling by adding 8 ounces (250 g) of egg noodles to the soup. In Chinese homes, a large bowl of this soup is often placed at the center of the table. Each person has a flat-bottomed soup spoon to dip into the bowl during the meal.

Utensils

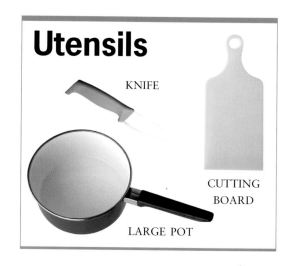

KNIFE

CUTTING BOARD

LARGE POT

TIPS & TRICKS

Experiment with different flavors for this soup. You can use a vegetable or seafood stock instead of chicken. You can also try using Chinese broccoli or **bok choy** *instead of the spinach. Be careful of your fingers when you cut the vegetables. Do not cut the vegetables too small either. You do not want them to become mushy while they are cooking.*

1 Cut the tomatoes, mushrooms, and carrots into bite-sized cubes. Hold the handle of the knife firmly in one hand and use the other hand to hold the vegetables. Keep your fingers away from the blade at all times.

2 Place the chicken stock and the carrots in a large pot. Bring the stock to a boil over medium heat. Simmer for about 5 minutes.

3 Add the spinach, mushrooms, and tomatoes. Stir carefully until the soup returns to a boil.

4 Add the soy sauce, salt, and sugar. Simmer for 1–2 minutes, then serve.

Ingredients

6 cups (1.5 l) chicken stock (made with boiling water and a bouillon cube)

2 fresh tomatoes

10 button mushrooms

2 small carrots

7 ounces (200 g) fresh spinach leaves

2 teaspoons light soy sauce

dash of sugar

dash of salt

Sweet and Sour Shrimp

Chinese cuisine can be divided into four major regions. Most of the early Chinese **immigrants** to the West came from the Canton region. North Americans are familiar with Cantonese Chinese food. The sweet and sour sauce in this recipe is a Cantonese sauce. It is also delicious with pork or chicken instead of shrimp.

1 Place the shrimp in a bowl with 2 tablespoons of the soy sauce. **Marinate** for 30 minutes.

2 Beat the egg in a small bowl. Using chopsticks or your fingers, dip the shrimp into the egg.

3 Place 3 tablespoons of the cornstarch on a plate. **Dredge** the shrimp in the cornstarch.

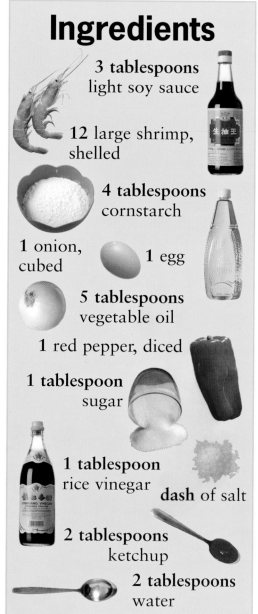

Ingredients

- **3 tablespoons** light soy sauce
- **12 large shrimp,** shelled
- **4 tablespoons** cornstarch
- **1 onion,** cubed
- **1 egg**
- **5 tablespoons** vegetable oil
- **1 red pepper, diced**
- **1 tablespoon** sugar
- **1 tablespoon** rice vinegar
- **dash** of salt
- **2 tablespoons** ketchup
- **2 tablespoons** water

4 Heat the oil in the wok. Add the shrimp and cook until they turn a pinkish orange. Be careful not to get splashed by the oil—have an adult help you. Use a slotted spoon to remove the shrimp. Place them on paper towels. Pour out most of the oil, except for 1 tablespoon.

13

5 Stir-fry the onion and red pepper for 2–3 minutes.

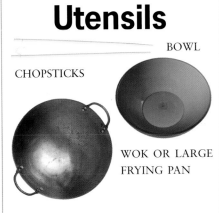

6 Place the cooked shrimp back in the wok and mix well.

Utensils

BOWL

CHOPSTICKS

WOK OR LARGE FRYING PAN

7 In a bowl, mix the remaining soy sauce, remaining cornstarch, salt, sugar, rice vinegar, ketchup, and water. Then add these ingredients to the wok and stir until the sauce is thick. Serve hot. You may top this dish with sliced oranges or spring onions.

Tofu with Pork

Tofu, also called bean curd, has a slightly nutty taste that blends in well with strong flavors. Tofu is made from soy milk and is very healthy. It is a common high-**protein** food in many parts of Asia, where less meat is eaten than in North America and Europe. You can find tofu in Asian supermarkets and health food stores.

1 Place the oil, garlic, and ginger in a wok on medium high heat. **Sauté** for 2 minutes. Now add the other ingredients except the pork, tofu, and onions and bring them to a boil.

2 When the sauce is bubbling, add the pork and cook for about 10 minutes, stirring continuously.

TIPS & TRICKS

The sauce that is made in step 1 can be prepared ahead of time and stored in the refrigerator until you need it. If you do not like pork, use chicken or beef instead.

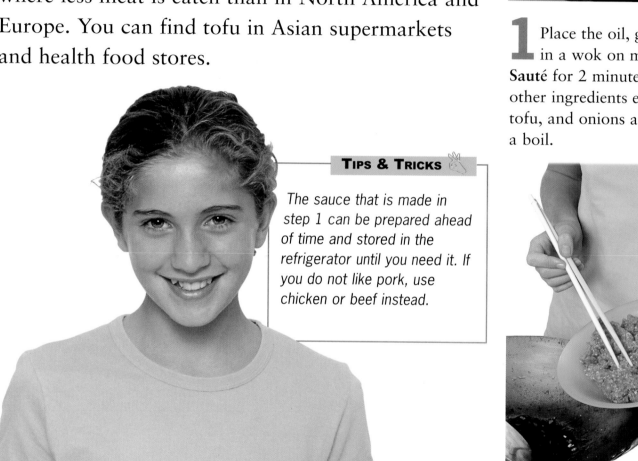

Utensils

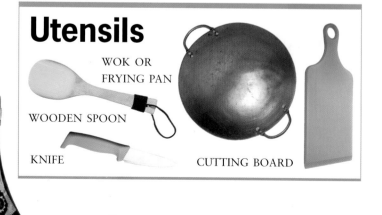

WOK OR FRYING PAN

WOODEN SPOON

KNIFE

CUTTING BOARD

3 Cut the tofu into bite-sized pieces and slice the green onions coarsely. Be sure to hold the knife firmly by the handle with one hand and hold the tofu and onions with your other hand. Keep your fingers away from the blade at all times.

4 Add the tofu to the wok and stir carefully.

5 Sprinkle with the green onions, and toss very carefully using chopsticks or a spoon. Serve hot.

Ingredients

1 clove garlic, minced

1 teaspoon ginger, minced

2 teaspoons light soy sauce

2 teaspoons dark soy sauce

1 teaspoon sesame oil

1 teaspoon sugar

dash of salt

dash of white pepper

1 teaspoon cornstarch

4 tablespoons water

½ pound (250 g) ground pork

1 pound (500 g) soft tofu

2 green onions

Braised Mushrooms

Chinese dried mushrooms can be found in Asian food stores and in many supermarkets. They come in plastic packages and need to be soaked in hot water before they are cooked. In this recipe, they are simmered in a sauce over low heat for 30 to 40 minutes. This cooking technique is called braising.

16

1 Soak the mushrooms in 2 cups (500 ml) of hot water for about 20 minutes. They should be soft.

Ingredients

20–25 large, Chinese dried mushrooms

3 cups (750 ml) hot water

1 tablespoon vegetable oil

1 clove garlic, minced

1 tablespoon light soy sauce

2 teaspoons sugar

4 tablespoons oyster sauce

Utensils

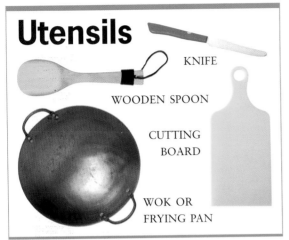

KNIFE

WOODEN SPOON

CUTTING
BOARD

WOK OR
FRYING PAN

2 Drain the mushrooms and dry them with a cloth. Use a table knife to cut off the stems.

3 Heat the oil in the wok and sauté the garlic over medium heat until it is soft.

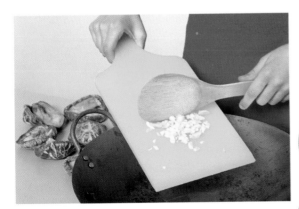

4 Add the soy sauce, oyster sauce, sugar, 1 cup (250 ml) hot water, and the mushrooms to the wok. Heat until the mixture is bubbling.

TIPS & TRICKS

If you can find them, mix some fresh shiitake mushrooms in with the dried mushrooms. They will give the dish an even better taste. Do not use button mushrooms in this dish. If the mushrooms are fresh, skip step 1. For added flavor, use chicken stock instead of water in the sauce.

5 Turn the heat down and cover part of the wok with a lid. Simmer until most of the liquid has **evaporated**. Serve hot.

Chinese New Year

The Chinese calendar is based on **lunar** and **solar** movements, the days and months are marked by the movements of the Sun and Moon. Chinese New Year falls on a different day each year because it is the day of the first new moon of the new year. Chinese New Year is probably the biggest and most important celebration in China, and it is celebrated by Chinese all over the world. Colors, food, and symbols all play a big part in making sure the New Year is full of good fortune. The celebration lasts 15 days and begins on New Year's Eve. On this evening, family members gather for a large dinner. New Year's Eve and New Year's Day are important to the family. Even if children have moved far away, they will try to come home for Chinese New Year. That is why the New Year's Eve dinner is also called the Reunion Dinner.

Children receive *hongbaos* at Chinese New Year. These are red envelopes filled with money and decorated with lucky symbols.

New Year's Cake

- 5 cups (1.25 l) **glutinous rice** flour
- 1⅔ cups (400 ml) brown sugar
- 1⅔ cups (400 ml) boiling water

Sift the flour (buy this special sticky flour at an Asian food store) into a large mixing bowl. Put the sugar in the boiling water and stir until it **dissolves**. Pour the water and sugar into the flour and mix well. Line an 8-inch (20 cm) Chinese steaming basket with parchment paper. Pour the mixture into the basket and make sure the top is level. Place the steaming basket over a pot of boiling water and steam for 2 hours. To test if the cake is cooked, stick a chopstick into the center. If it comes out dry, the cake is ready. Turn the cooked cake over and remove the paper. When cool, wrap in foil and refrigerate for two days before cutting into four- or six-sided shapes.

There are many foods that are eaten during Chinese New Year. A large amount of food is prepared to show that the family will have good fortune in the coming year. All the dishes have special meanings. For example, chicken stands for prosperity and fish represents togetherness and plenty. Desserts are also popular and represent a happy life. One favorite dessert is *tang yuan*, a dumpling made of glutinous rice flour rolled into balls and stuffed with a sweet filling of peanuts or sesame seeds. This is commonly eaten on the last day of the Chinese New Year.

A New Year Legend

Most people agree that the Chinese word *Nian*, which means "year," was the name of a monster that ate people on New Year's Eve. The people were scared of Nian but an old man came to their rescue. He told Nian, "I have heard of your ferocious power, but can you swallow the beasts of prey on Earth instead of helpless humans?" The monster agreed and stopped eating people. The old man told people to put up red paper decorations on their windows and doors at each year's end. The color red would scare away Nian. Even today, the Chinese hang red paper decorations during New Year's celebrations.

Orange is the color of good luck. On Chinese New Year, bring two mandarin oranges for your host. You will also receive two oranges when you leave.

Vegetables with Oyster Sauce

Lightly boiled or steamed vegetables are a common part of Chinese cuisine. Make sure that these vegetables are crisp and not overcooked. They will taste better and are better for you. Overcooked vegetables can lose some of their vitamins.

TIPS & TRICKS

For a sauce with more flavor, slice a green onion thinly and sauté it in 1 tablespoon of vegetable oil and sesame oil. Drizzle the oil and onions over the vegetables.

1 Fill a large pot half full with cold water and a dash of salt. Place it over high heat and boil.

2 When the water is boiling, add the vegetables. Do not cook them too long. The vegetables should still be crisp and have a good crunch to them.

3 Take the vegetables out using a pair of chopsticks or tongs. Shake off the extra water.

4 Arrange the vegetables nicely on a serving dish. Pour the oyster sauce over the top and serve hot. Try topping them with sesame seeds as well.

Utensils

LARGE POT

CHOPSTICKS
OR TONGS

Ingredients

dash of salt

6 to 8 stalks green leafy vegetable, such as bok choy

2 tablespoons oyster sauce

Chinese Omelette

Eggs are not usually served as a main dish in Chinese cooking. This style of omelette, however, has become popular. It is quick and easy to prepare and can be served at breakfast, lunch, or dinner. Try adding your own favorite foods to this omelette.

Utensils

CHOPSTICKS

BOWL

SPATULA

SKILLET OR FRYING PAN

1 Combine the onion, meat, soy sauce, and salt in a mixing bowl. Mix until it is smooth and without large lumps.

2 Beat the eggs in a separate bowl until they are light and frothy. Add the egg to the meat and onion mixture.

Ingredients

1 small white onion, chopped

¼ pound (125 g) diced ham

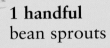

1 handful bean sprouts

½ tablespoon light soy sauce

2 eggs

1 teaspoon salt

2 green onions, chopped

2 tablespoons vegetable oil

For the sauce

½ cup (125 ml) chicken stock

2 teaspoons thick soy sauce

dash of sugar

2 teaspoons cornstarch

3 Heat the oil in a frying pan and slowly pour in all the egg mixture. When the omelette gets a little puffy and the underside is golden brown, add the bean sprouts and spring onions. Flip the omelette over and cook until the other side is brown too.

TIPS & TRICKS

Try using crabmeat or diced roast pork instead of the ham in this recipe. When cooking the omelette, let the sides set and then push them toward the center of the pan. Tip the pan and let the extra egg mixture flow to the sides. Your omelette will cook more evenly and it will be easier to turn over. Also shake the pan while cooking to make the omelette fluffier.

4 As the omelette is cooking, mix all the ingredients for the sauce together in a saucepan and bring to a boil. Pour the sauce over the omelette or serve separately.

23

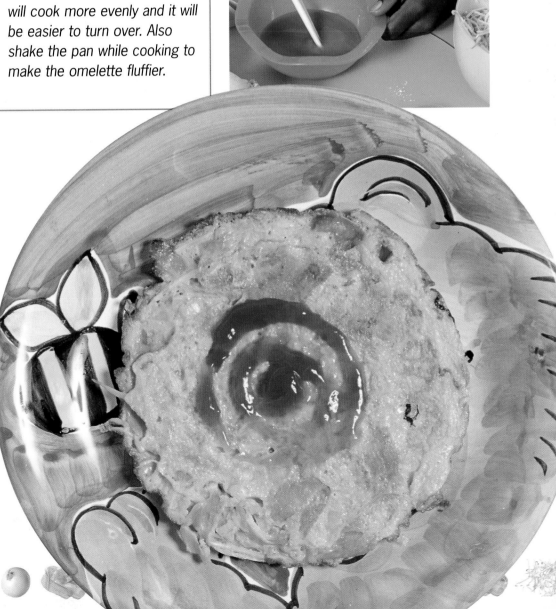

Fried Rice

This dish is very popular at Chinese restaurants. Usually fried rice is served in Chinese homes as a one-dish meal, although it is also used instead of steamed rice to go with a meal. At special banquets, fried rice is served toward the end of the meal to fill up anyone who did not get enough to eat!

Utensils

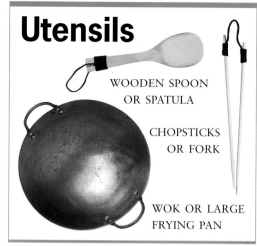

WOODEN SPOON OR SPATULA

CHOPSTICKS OR FORK

WOK OR LARGE FRYING PAN

Ingredients

½ **pound** (250 g) chopped ham or cooked shrimp

1 egg

1 cup (250 ml) fresh or **thawed** frozen vegetables (corn, peas, and carrots)

4 cups (1 l) cooked long-grain rice

2 cloves garlic, finely chopped

1 tablespoon light soy sauce

2 tablespoons vegetable oil

1 Add 1 tablespoon (15 ml) of the oil to the wok then place over medium heat.

2 Add the garlic and stir-fry until it turns pale golden brown. Be careful not to burn the garlic because it will make the dish taste bitter.

3 Add the ham or shrimp together with the vegetables to the wok. Stir-fry for 1 minute.

4 Add the rice and stir-fry until all the ingredients are well mixed. Place the rice mixture on a plate. Add the remaining oil to the wok.

5 Beat the egg in a bowl, then add it to the wok. Stir with a fork or chopsticks to scramble the egg. When cooked, put the rice mixture back into the wok. Pour the soy sauce on top and stir-fry until well mixed. Serve hot.

TIPS & TRICKS

Fried rice should not be sticky, the grains should be separate and dry. To get dry rice, use rice left over from the day before. If you do not have any rice from last night's dinner, make sure that the rice you use is cooked and left to cool before you start preparing your fried rice.

Long-Life Noodles

Noodles are popular in Chinese cuisine. They are always served at birthday parties because long noodles are believed to be symbols of long life. To have a long life, people try to eat the noodles whole, without biting through them. Eating noodles whole takes quite a bit of practice, so make this dish often!

2 Heat the oil in a wok. When it is hot, stir-fry the minced ginger and garlic until golden brown.

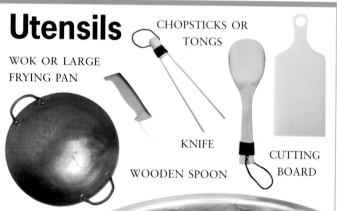

Utensils

CHOPSTICKS OR TONGS

WOK OR LARGE FRYING PAN

KNIFE

WOODEN SPOON

CUTTING BOARD

1 If using dried noodles, follow the instructions on the package to cook them. Drain and set aside.

3 Add the pork and stir-fry until it is well cooked and pale gold.

TIPS & TRICKS

To avoid having the noodles stick together before cooking, toss them in a little oil. Then lay them on a plate until you need them. Stir the noodles with care after adding them to the wok to avoid breaking them. If you cannot find a fish cake in an Asian supermarket, use cooked shrimp instead. If you cannot find fresh bean sprouts, thinly sliced Chinese cabbage works well. Both vegetables give a crunch to the dish and balance out the soft noodles.

Ingredients

8 ounces (250 g) fresh or dried egg noodles

2 tablespoons vegetable oil

1 teaspoon ginger, minced

2–3 cloves garlic, minced

3½ ounces (100 g) sliced pork

4 cups (100 g) bean sprouts

3½ ounces (100 g) sliced fish cake

1 tablespoon light soy sauce

1 tablespoon oyster sauce

5 Add the noodles to the wok and stir-fry another 2 to 3 minutes.

4 Add the bean sprouts and fish cake and stir-fry for 2 to 3 minutes more.

6 Pour in the soy sauce and oyster sauce, and stir-fry until all the ingredients are well mixed. Serve hot.

MEDIUM EGG NOODLES

Red-Bean Soup

In Chinese cuisine, sweet soups are often served as a dessert at the end of the meal. While red-bean soup is not common in Chinese restaurants, it is one of the most popular desserts in Chinese homes. Best of all, this sweet soup is easy to make!

TIPS & TRICKS

*To add more flavor to this dish, try adding some shredded orange **zest** to the soup as it is cooking.*

1 Soak the beans in a large bowl of cold water overnight.

2 The next day, boil a large pot of water. Drain the beans and add them to the boiling water.

3 Cook the beans for about 1½ hours, until they are soft. If you like firmer beans, cook them for a shorter time.

4 Stir in the sugar and cook for 5 to 10 minutes more. Serve the soup hot.

Ingredients

5 cups (1¼ l) cold water

1 cup (250 ml) dried red beans

about ½ cup (125 ml) sugar

Utensils

WOODEN SPOON

LARGE POT

Egg Custard Tarts

Egg custard tarts are the perfect way to finish a Chinese meal. The egg custard tarts are usually made with a flaky pastry. We use store-bought pastry here, use the brand that you like best.

Ingredients

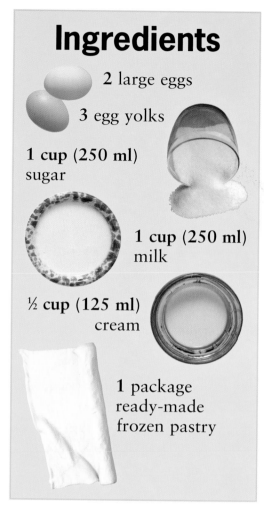

2 large eggs

3 egg yolks

1 cup (250 ml) sugar

1 cup (250 ml) milk

½ cup (125 ml) cream

1 package ready-made frozen pastry

1 Preheat the oven to 300 °F (150 °C).

Utensils

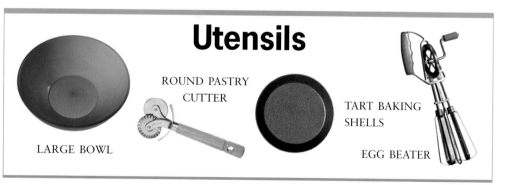

LARGE BOWL

ROUND PASTRY CUTTER

TART BAKING SHELLS

EGG BEATER

2 Combine the egg yolks and whole eggs in a jug or bowl. Beat them slowly with the egg beater.

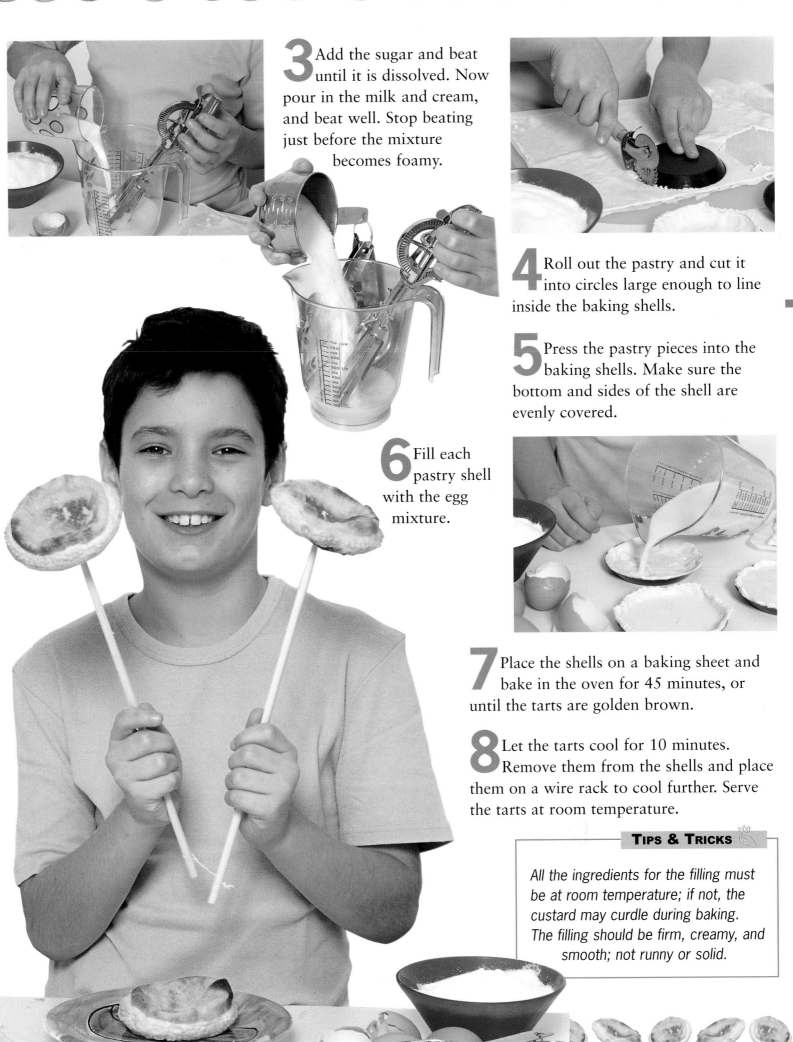

3 Add the sugar and beat until it is dissolved. Now pour in the milk and cream, and beat well. Stop beating just before the mixture becomes foamy.

4 Roll out the pastry and cut it into circles large enough to line inside the baking shells.

5 Press the pastry pieces into the baking shells. Make sure the bottom and sides of the shell are evenly covered.

6 Fill each pastry shell with the egg mixture.

7 Place the shells on a baking sheet and bake in the oven for 45 minutes, or until the tarts are golden brown.

8 Let the tarts cool for 10 minutes. Remove them from the shells and place them on a wire rack to cool further. Serve the tarts at room temperature.

TIPS & TRICKS

All the ingredients for the filling must be at room temperature; if not, the custard may curdle during baking. The filling should be firm, creamy, and smooth; not runny or solid.

Glossary

appetizer (A-pih-ty-zur) A dish served before the main course.

bok choy (BOK CHOY) A green leafy Chinese vegetable.

Cantonese (kan-tuh-NEEZ) Native to the Canton region of southern China.

cuisine (kwih-ZEEN) A style of cooking.

diced (DYST) Cut into tiny cubes using a knife.

dissolves (dih-ZOLVZ) When something, such as salt, mixes into a liquid, such as water.

dredge (DREJ) To cover food in a substance such as flour or starch.

evaporated (ih-VA-puh-rayt-ed) When a liquid, such as water, is heated until it turns into a gas.

glutinous rice (GLOOT-nus RYS) Rice that is sticky and thick when it is cooked.

heaping (HEEP-ing) Describing a measurement that is slightly larger than usual.

immigrants (IH-muh-grunts) People who have left their native country to live in a new one.

lunar (LOO-ner) Relating to the Moon.

marinate (MER-uh-nayt) To let food sit in a liquid mixture.

minced (MINTST) Finely chopped.

protein (PROH-teen) A substance found in foods such as meat and beans needed by all living things.

sauté (saw-TAY) To quickly fry food in a small amount of oil.

solar (SOH-ler) Relating to the Sun.

thawed (THAHD) Changed from solid to liquid by warming.

tofu (TOH-foo) A protein-rich food made from soybeans.

wonton (WON-ton) A small dumpling made of a rice-noodle sheet wrapped around food.

zest (ZEST) Shredded peel of citrus fruits, such as oranges or lemons.

Index

Web Sites

Due to the changing nature of Internet links, PowerKids Press has developed an online list of Web sites related to the subject of this book. This site is updated regularly. Please use this link to access the list: www.powerkidslinks.com/lgc/chinese/